FABLES: THE DARK AGES

FABLES: THE DARK AGES

FABLES CREATED BY BILL WILLINGHAM

Bill Willingham
writer

Mark Buckingham
Peter Gross
Andrew Pepoy
Michael Allred
David Hahn
artists

Lee Loughridge
Laura Allred
colorists

Todd Klein
letterer

James Jean (#76-81)
Mark Buckingham (#82)
original series covers

KAREN BERGER
Senior VP-Executive Editor

SHELLY BOND
Editor-original series

ANGELA RUFINO
Associate Editor-original series

SCOTT NYBAKKEN
Editor-collected edition

ROBBIN BROSTERMAN
Senior Art Director

PAUL LEVITZ
President & Publisher

GEORG BREWER
VP-Design & DC Direct Creative

RICHARD BRUNING
Senior VP-Creative Director

PATRICK CALDON
Executive VP-Finance & Operations

CHRIS CARAMALIS
VP-Finance

JOHN CUNNINGHAM
VP-Marketing

TERRI CUNNINGHAM
VP-Managing Editor

AMY GENKINS
Senior VP-Business & Legal Affairs

ALISON GILL
VP-Manufacturing

DAVID HYDE
VP-Publicity

HANK KANALZ
VP-General Manager, WildStorm

JIM LEE
Editorial Director-WildStorm

GREGORY NOVECK
Senior VP-Creative Affairs

SUE POHJA
VP-Book Trade Sales

STEVE ROTTERDAM
Senior VP-Sales & Marketing

CHERYL RUBIN
Senior VP-Brand Management

ALYSSE SOLL
VP-Advertising & Custom Publishing

JEFF TROJAN
VP-Business Development, DC Direct

BOB WAYNE
VP-Sales

*This volume is dedicated to Stacy Sinner,
who went into the woods, found my
house of many stories there,
and then built it for me.*
— Bill Willingham

In loving memory of Marisa, Irma's Mum.
— Mark Buckingham

Cover illustration by James Jean
Logo design by Brainchild Studios/NYC

FABLES: THE DARK AGES

Published by DC Comics. Cover and compilation
Copyright © 2009 DC Comics.
All Rights Reserved.

Originally published in single magazine form
as FABLES 76-82. Copyright © 2008, 2009
Bill Willingham and DC Comics.
All Rights Reserved. All characters, their
distinctive likenesses and related elements
featured in this publication are trademarks of
Bill Willingham. VERTIGO is a trademark of
DC Comics. The stories, characters and incidents
featured in this publication are entirely fictional.
DC Comics does not read or accept unsolicited
submissions of ideas, stories or artwork.

DC Comics, 1700 Broadway, New York, NY 10019
A Warner Bros. Entertainment Company.
Printed in the USA. Second Printing.
ISBN: 978-1-4012-2316-8

SUSTAINABLE FORESTRY INITIATIVE

**Certified Fiber
Sourcing**

www.sfiprogram.org

Fiber used in this product line meets the sourcing requirements
of the SFI program. www.sfiprogram.org SGS-SFICOC-0130

Table of Contents

WHO'S WHO IN FABLETOWN

PINOCCHIO

Geppetto's first son, and quite possibly the only person in hundreds of worlds who still has any love for the mean old ma[...]

GEPPETTO

He was once Fabletown's most terrible adversary. Now he's one of them.

BEAUTY AND BEAST

They help run Fabletown as the deputy mayor and sheriff, respectively.

GRIMBLE

The Woodland's perpetually sleepy security officer and perhaps the most famous (and infamous) of all bridge trolls.

BIGBY

The Big Bad Wolf, reformed now and happily married.

SNOW WHITE

Bigby's wife and still a power in Fabletown politics.

BAGHEERA

One of Mowgli's closest friends and advisors.

BOY BLUE

A wicked horn player and a warrior of note. One of the heroes of the war against the Empire, where he received a wound to his arm.

DOCTOR SWINEHEART

The best military surgeon in uncountable worlds, and Boy Blue's postwar physician.

NURSE SPRAT

Jack Sprat's widow, and not the nicest of ladies.

ROSE RED

She still runs the Farm and recently turned dow[...] Boy Blue's ill-timed romantic overtures.

FLYCATCHER

The famous janitor king and former Frog Prince.

SINBAD

A leader of Fabletown East (in the Homelands' version of Baghdad) and a hero of the war against the Empire.

FRAU TOTENKINDER

The Black Forest Witch and leader of Fabletown's magic set.

MOWGLI

A hunter of no small repute, and one of Fabletown's top secret agents.

BIGBY'S BROTHERS

Six bad siblings, sometimes wolves, sometimes monsters, and sometimes fish.

KING COLE

Once the beloved mayor of Fabletown, then not, then mayor again.

BUFKIN

A flying monkey from Oz who knows where the books go.

BABA YAGA

Less than a handful of Fables know she's being held captive somewhere in the back warrens of the Woodland's business office.

COLIN THE PIG

Once one of the Three Little Pigs, he's now just a big dead pig head on a stick, but one with some sort of oracular power.

THE STORY SO FAR

After spending centuries as a hidden community in exile, Fabletown finally rose up in righteous anger and brought down Geppetto's vast empire in a quick and nearly bloodless war — though victory cid have some costs, including the loss of Prince Charming, who sacrificed himself to save the day. Now, due to some deft eleventh-hour political maneuvering on Pinocchio's part, their feared and hated Adversary is Fabletown's newest member.

AROUND THE TOWN

IN WHICH THE NEWEST MEMBER OF FABLETOWN GETS A LOOK AROUND HIS NEW HOME AND THE GOOD PEOPLE OF FABLETOWN GET THEIR FIRST LOOK AT HIM IN RETURN

OUTRAGEOUS HOOLIGANISM, *THAT'S* WHAT IT IS!

AFTER ALL, IT'S NOT AS IF THEY'RE ACCUSING YOU OF SOMETHING YOU DIDN'T ACTUALLY DO.

YOUR HANDS *DO* HAVE AN AWFUL LOT OF *BLOOD* ON THEM-- FIGURATIVELY SPEAKING OF COURSE.

SETTLE DOWN, YOU LOT!

THERE'S GOING TO BE NO VIOLENCE HERE.

UNLESS YOU'RE PREPARED TO DEAL WITH THE THREE OF US IN OUR MORE *FORMIDABLE* ASPECTS.

UHM... MAYBE WE SHOULD START OUR TOUR DOWN AT *THIS* END OF THE STREET, POPS.

I DIDN'T *THINK* SO.

AND SEE THAT PRETTY LADY OVER THERE, POPS? THAT'S SNOW WHITE.

SHE BASICALLY *RUNS* FABLETOWN.

UHM...THAT'S NOT ENTIRELY TRUE ANYMORE. YOU'VE BEEN GONE FOR SOME TIME, PINOCCHIO, SO YOU'RE NOT CAUGHT UP ON RECENT CHANGES.

BUT NOW MY *WIFE*--

OOPS, THAT'S RIGHT. SORRY, POPS, LET ME *CORRECT* MYSELF.

SNOW WHITE *USED* TO RUN FABLETOWN FOR YEARS AND YEARS, AND NOW SHE ONLY RUNS IT WHENEVER SHE WANTS TO.

HRRUMMPH.

SNOW WHITE? I KNOW THAT NAME....

YOU! YOUNG *MISSY!* COME OVER HERE!

NOW, MR. GEPPETTO, LET ME REMIND YOU AGAIN.

YOU CAN NO LONGER SIMPLY *ORDER* PEOPLE AROUND. THOSE DAYS ARE OVER.

GOOD MORNING, GENTLEMEN. THAT CROWD BACK THERE GIVE YOU ANY TROUBLE?

NOTHING WE COULDN'T DEFLATE WITH A DEFTLY CHOSEN WORD OR TWO.

SO, WOMAN, I UNDERSTAND YOU'RE THE ONE WHO *WILLINGLY* LIES DOWN WITH THIS CUR.

DISGUSTING.

EXCUSE ME?

AND NOW THEY SAY YOU LARGELY *RAN* THE WAR AGAINST ME.

WHY?

DID YOU EVER THINK TO COUNT THE *COST*?

MORE THAN TWO HUNDRED HERETOFORE PEACEFUL AND ORDERLY WORLDS ARE SUDDENLY *LEADERLESS.* I IMAGINE THE LOCAL UPRISINGS MAY HAVE ALREADY BEGUN.

SUCH BLOODLETTING THERE WILL BE. THE COMING DEATH TOLL WILL NUMBER IN THE--WELL, WHO CAN *SAY* ACCURATELY?

HAVE FUN OUT IN THE MUNDY.

WE WILL. WE'VE GOT A WHOLE BIG DAY PLANNED.

Espresso

TAXI

MUND-E

ARE YOU SURE YOU DON'T NEED ME TO GO WITH? THIS IS THEIR FIRST FULL TRIAL AS *NORMAL* KIDS. I COULD ALWAYS TELL KING COLE TO DO WITHOUT ME.

NONSENSE. GO TO YOUR MEETING. WE'LL BE FINE. THESE CUBS ARE TRAINED BY NOW, OR THEY'LL *NEVER* BE. AND WE'LL ALL BE PERFECTLY SAFE WITH GHOST ALONG.

HAVE FUN!

MIND YOUR *MOTHER!*

TAXI

MUND-E

GREEN T SHO

HOW ABOUT SOME CANDY, POPS? ON ME.

OH, I WOULDN'T WORRY TOO MUCH ABOUT THAT, BEAUTY.

THE AMNESTY ONLY COVERS THE ATROCITIES HE'S COMMITTED SO FAR.

SOONER RATHER THAN LATER, HE'LL COMMIT SOME *NEW* CRIME. BY NOW IT'S IN HIS NATURE.

SLOWLY, KING COLE. SLOWLY.

SINCE IT'S IMPORTANT THAT HE NEVER SUSPECT WE'RE DOING IT, WE HAVE TO TREAD CAREFULLY, MY COLLEAGUES AND I.

THEN WE CAN *AX* THE OLD DUFFER WITH A CLEAR CONSCIENCE.

ASSUMING WE'RE ACTUALLY *ABLE* TO KILL HIM. FRAU TOTENKINDER, HOW GOES THE EFFORT TO DISMANTLE HIS MAGICAL PROTECTIONS?

SPEAKING OF THINGS HE SHOULD NEVER SUSPECT, WHEN IS OUR ALL-SEEING *BLIND MAN* GOING TO GET A LOOK AT HIM?

AMNESTY OR NOT, WE NEED TO KNOW THE FULL EXTENT OF HIS PAST MISDEEDS.

AND THE NATURE OF ANY SURVIVING IMPERIAL POWERS ARRAYING AGAINST US.

THE BOYS SHOULD BE ACCIDENTALLY RUNNING INTO KAY ANY MINUTE NOW.

YOU!

I DIDN'T *BELIEVE* IT, BUT HERE YOU ARE!

THEY ACTUALLY LET YOU *IN!*

NOW, HOLD ON, MRS. CORNHUSK. WE CAN'T ALLOW YOU TO--

MY HUSBAND *DIED* FIGHTING THE INVASION OF OUR LAND.

AND TO *PUNISH* US YOUR SOLDIERS KILLED MY PARENTS, MY SPINSTER SISTER, AND ALL SEVEN OF MY CHILDREN!

SO WHAT?

THIS ISN'T THE *TIME,* MA'AM.

ONLY I LIVED, BECAUSE I WAS AWAY AT MARKET.

AGAIN, SO *WHAT?*

MILLIONS DIED AS I CARVED OUT MY EMPIRE. MILLIONS MORE WERE DELIVERED INTO DIRE BONDAGE, WHERE THEY CERTAINLY DIDN'T SURVIVE LONG.

BUT THAT RESULTED IN A LIFE OF PEACE AND SECURITY FOR UNTOLD BILLIONS THAT SPANNED MANY CENTURIES.

WHO ELSE HAS EVER ACCOMPLISHED SO MUCH? WHEN AGAIN WILL SO MANY ENJOY SUCH WIDESPREAD SAFETY FOR SO LONG?

YOU'RE A MONSTER! A BLOODY-HANDED MONSTER!

OF COURSE.

NO KIND MAN COULD EVER DO WHAT I'VE DONE. THE COMPASSIONATE MAN WILL LET BILLIONS SUFFER AND DIE, AS LONG AS HE DOESN'T HAVE TO GET HIS HANDS DIRTY.

MADAM, MY HEART TRULY GOES OUT TO YOU, BUT YOU REALLY DO HAVE TO GO AWAY NOW. THERE, THERE, THAT'S A GOOD LADY.

GOD WILL JUDGE YOU, GEPPETTO! MARK MY WORDS!

IF HE DOES, HE'LL THINK HE'S LOOKING INTO A MIRROR.

WELL NOW, WASN'T THAT SOMETHING?

THESE SWEETS HAVE MADE ME HUNGRY FOR SOMETHING MORE SUBSTANTIAL.

ANYONE ELSE READY FOR LUNCH?

ISN'T THAT A RESTAURANT BEHIND US? WHY DON'T WE EAT THERE?

TRUTH BE TOLD, MY SON'S COOKING DOESN'T APPEAL TO ME.

COMING?

ABSOLUTELY *NOT!*

BUT, VULCO! HE'S A MEMBER OF FABLETOWN NOW!

SO WHAT?

ALL THAT MEANS IS I HAVE TO PUT UP WITH HIM LIVING IN OUR COMMUNITY, AND I'M NOT SUPPOSED TO *BRING UP* HIS PAST CRIMES. YOU'LL NOTICE I DIDN'T MENTION ONE OF THEM.

MANAGEMENT RESER RIGHT TO REFUSE S OR ANY REASON

BUT NOTHING IN FABLETOWN LAW REQUIRES ME TO *FEED* HIM, OR EVEN *ALLOW* HIM INTO MY DINER.

SEE THAT NOTICE? "THE MANAGEMENT"--THAT'S ME-- "RESERVES THE RIGHT TO REFUSE SERVICE FOR ANY REASON."

MANAGEMENT RESERVES
THE RIGHT TO REFUSE SERVICE
OR ANY REASON

AND UNLIKE OUT IN THE MUNDY, OUR PRIVATE POLICIES STILL HAVE SOME *TOOTH* BEHIND THEM. YOU CAN'T SUE ME FOR MAKING YOU *FEEL* BAD.

AND DON'T BOTHER TRYING THE BRANSTOCK, OR THE YELLOW BRICK ROADHOUSE NEITHER.

WE'VE ALREADY PLEDGED TO STAND *TOGETHER* ON THIS.

GO OUT INTO THE *MUNDY* IF YOU'RE HUNGRY, OLD MAN. YOU'LL NEVER FIND SO MUCH AS A *CRUMB* TO EAT HERE--NOT AS LONG AS *I* OWN THE EGGMAN.

BRANST TAVERN

GLASS SLIPPER SHOP

--IMPUDENT BOY SHOULD BE *HORSEWHIPPED*, SINCE YOU'RE ALL SO SQUEAMISH ABOUT EXECUTING YOUR LAWLESS RUFFIANS. *MY* MONEY'S AS GOOD AS ANYBODY'S.

ACTUALLY, YOU DON'T *HAVE* ANY MONEY, POPS. NOT YET. BUT I WAS GOING TO PAY.

MANAGEMENT RESERVES THE RIGHT TO REFUSE SERVICE FOR...

OOPS! EXCUSE ME! I DIDN'T SEE--

YOU SHOULD *WATCH* WHERE YOU'RE GOING!

WELL, HE DOES SEEM TO BE *BLIND*, POPS.

WHAT KIND OF BODYGUARDS ARE YOU THREE, IF ANYONE AT ALL CAN SIMPLY *WALK* RIGHT INTO ME?

OH MY.

WHAT NOW? ARE YOU *DRUNK*, BOY? ARE YOU TOUCHED IN THE HEAD?

YOU--

WE USED TO *EXECUTE* OUR IMBECILES BACK IN THE EMPIRE, TO KEEP THEM FROM BREEDING MORE OF THEIR KIND.

YOU FOLKS NO DOUBT *CELEBRATE* THEM.

....SO MANY...

SO MANY....

WELL, THIS DAY COULD HAVE GONE BETTER, I SUPPOSE.

BUT IT WASN'T A TOTAL DISASTER. NO ONE QUITE *LYNCHED* US, AND WHO KNOWS? IN A FEW WEEKS THEY MIGHT ACTUALLY GET USED TO SEEING US EVERY DAY.

SO, POPS, WHAT DO YOU WANT TO DO TOMORROW?

I WAS THINKING WE MIGHT WANT TO VENTURE OUT INTO THE MUNDY.

IT'S A REALLY GREAT CITY AND WE WON'T NEED THE BODYGUARDS OUT THERE, SINCE THE MUNDYS DON'T KNOW YOU FROM ADAM.

THEY HAVE SOME AMAZING RESTAURANTS, AND A GREAT BIG PARK, AND WE COULD GO SIGHTSEEING.

OOH, THEY EVEN HAVE AN AIR-CRAFT CARRIER--A REAL ONE--THAT WE CAN GO ON AND LOOK AT ALL OF THE FIGHTER JETS AND BOMBERS AND STUFF. WOULDN'T *THAT* BE COOL?

YOU COULD SEE ALL THE EVIDENCE FIRST HAND ON WHY WE'D NEVER HAVE BEEN ABLE TO CONQUER THE MUNDY WORLD. OH, HOW THEY WOULD HAVE *SO* KICKED OUR ASSES!

HRRMPH!

NEXT: LIFE AFTER EMPIRE

IN ANY CASE, IT'S *LOOT* I'M AFTER-- NOT MOURNING A CORRUPT KING WHO WAS ALWAYS TOO READY TO DO THE FAR EMPEROR'S BIDDING.

WELL, WE'LL FIND NO TREASURE HERE.

MY FRIEND, WE ARRIVED TOO LATE TO GET A PORTION OF ANY BOOTY KEPT HERE.

SO WHERE DO WE GO TO GET OUR FAIR SHARE?

THE LEGENDARY MERCENARY TEAM OF FREDDY AND MOUSE CAN HARDLY BE THE *ONLY* ONES TO MISS OUT ON THE LOOTING IN THESE TROUBLED TIMES.

WHOEVER MADE THIS MESS, RETIRING THE PREVIOUS REGIME, WILL ALREADY HAVE PICKED THE PALACE *CLEAN.*

WHERE WOULD OUR VAUNTED REPUTATIONS BE *THEN?*

THERE'S A HIDDEN ROAD THAT GOES UP INTO THE MOUNTAINS FROM HERE. IT LEADS TO A SMALL FORT FEW KNOW ABOUT--

--FORT RESOLVE, OR SOMETHING LIKE THAT.

THEN, BY ALL MEANS, FREDDY, LET'S BE ON OUR WAY, WITH ALL EXPEDIENCY.

AND DEPRIVE THE CROWS AND OTHER SCAVENGERS OF THEIR SHARE OF THE *SPOILS?* LORD FORFEND.

YOU DON'T WANT TO BURY OLD CUPPERHAND FIRST? AFTER ALL, HE WAS OUR KING FOR THE PAST TWENTY YEARS. BAD AS HE WAS, WE EARNED GOOD WAGES IN HIS EMPLOY.

I WAS ONE OF THE GUARDS ON A MULE CARAVAN ONCE THAT TOOK A PRETTY HUGE LOAD OF TREASURE UP THERE.

I'D HAZARD THE FREEDOM-LOVING REBELS HAVEN'T THOUGHT OF HEADING UP THERE YET. TOO MANY LOWLAND CITIES STILL TO LIBERATE.

AND JUST A FEW BLOCKS ACROSS TOWN...

ALL WE WANT IS OUR GUNS BACK, BEAUTY, AND A LIFT FROM BOY BLUE TO ONE OF THE EMPIRE WORLDS, WHERE WE CAN CARVE OUT OUR OWN HUMBLE PIECE OF A VERY BIG *PIE.*

BLUE AND THE WITCHING CLOAK AREN'T AVAILABLE FOR NOW, MR. BROOM. AND THEY AREN'T *YOUR* GUNS. THEY BELONG TO FABLETOWN.

BUT YOU CAN'T JUST MAKE *WARRIOR-KILLERS* OF US AND THEN CAST US ASIDE!

DO YOU HAVE THAT LIST OF CARS GOING UP TO THE FARM FOR PRINCE CHARMING'S MEMORIAL, HONEY? I NEED TO MATCH DRIVERS WITH PASSENGERS.

IT'S ALREADY ON YOUR *DESK,* SWEETIE. TOP OF YOUR IN-BOX.

THANKS, PUMPKIN.

WE'RE THE S.O.S.! THE *SOCIETY OF SECONDS!* AND I'M OUR ELECTED *SPOKES-MAN.*

SO? THAT SUPPOSED TO *MEAN* ANYTHING TO ME?

WE'RE THE SECOND, THIRD AND *FOURTH* GENERATION FABLES-- AND SO ON--WHO WERE BORN HERE IN THE MUNDY WORLD AND DON'T HAVE SPECIFIC HOMELANDS TO RETURN TO.

WE JUST WANT A CHANCE TO CARVE OUT HOMELANDS OF OUR OWN. WE FOUGHT *YOUR* WAR OF REVENGE AND LIBERATION, SO NOW WE SHOULD RIGHTFULLY *SHARE* IN THE SPOILS.

ALL THINGS IN TIME. BIGBY'S IN CHARGE OF THE HOMELAND RECOVERY PROGRAM, NOW THAT PRINCE CHARMING IS...UHM...IS GONE.

IF YOU CAN CONVINCE *HIM* TO GIVE YOU GUNS AND THEN TURN YOU LOOSE TO CONQUER AN INNOCENT WORLD, TO START YOUR OWN EVIL LITTLE EMPIRES, THEN YOU'VE *MY* BLESSING TOO.

THAT'S *HARDLY* A FAIR DESCRIPTION OF WHAT WE HAVE IN MIND!

DON'T WASTE TIME ON ME. CONVINCE *BIGBY.* IF YOU LIKE I'LL RESERVE YOU A SEAT ON TODAY'S TRANSPORT UP THERE, TO PLEAD YOUR CASE.

NEVER MIND.

BUT MARK MY *WORDS,* MISS DEPUTY MAYOR! YOU HAVEN'T HEARD THE *LAST* FROM THE S.O.S.!

DID YOU FIND THE LIST, SHERIFF?

YEP. RIGHT WHERE YOU LEFT IT. SO, NEXT ITEM: WE NEED TO SETTLE THE DEBATE ON THE ACTUAL MEMORIAL SYMBOL.

DO WE WANT A BIG STONE OBELISK OR THE LIFE-SIZE BRONZE STATUE?

MY VOTE IS FOR THE OBELISK. NO SCULPTOR IN EXISTENCE, MUNDY OR FABLE, COULD *POSSIBLY* CAPTURE CHARMING'S TRUE LIKENESS.

OH?

YOU KNOW--THAT SIZZLING, SULTRY *SOME-THING* HE ALWAYS RADIATED, THAT TRANSCENDED WHAT MERE *PHOTOGRAPHS* COULD DUPLICATE.

YOU'RE NOT GOING TO MAKE ME FEEL GUILTY ABOUT SERVING IN KING CUPPERHAND'S ARMY, FREDDY, NO MATTER *HOW* VILE HE WAS.

WE'RE MERCENARIES. AND WHAT IS A MERCENARY'S HIGHEST DUTY?

TO GET PAID.

EXACTLY RIGHT--AND TO LIVE LONG ENOUGH TO *SPEND* THAT PAY.

NOW, WE HAD A CHOICE TO FIGHT WITH THE KING OR AGAINST HIM.

BUT SINCE THE KING HAD THE BACKING OF THE EMPIRE, THOSE WHO FOUGHT AGAINST HIM TENDED TO DIE--IN QUITE *REMARKABLE* NUMBERS.

I KNOW YOU KNOW THIS BECAUSE YOU'VE *REMARKED* UPON IT MORE THAN ONCE.

HOWEVER, THOSE WHO FOUGHT *WITH* THE KING GENERALLY SURVIVED TO SPEND THEIR PAY.

CASE CLOSED, MY HIRSUTE FRIEND. WE WERE LEGALLY AND MORALLY IN THE RIGHT.

LOOK THERE. I THINK I SPY THE FORT AHEAD. LOOSEN YOUR SWORD, MOUSE. WE MAY HAVE TO *FIGHT* OUR WAY IN.

FABLETOWN.

SIT DOWN, GEPPETTO. MAKE YOURSELF COMFORTABLE. POUR YOURSELF SOME *TEA* IF YOU LIKE.

WHAT DO YOU *WANT* FROM ME, OLD WOMAN?

I THOUGHT IT WAS TIME WE MET, FACE TO FACE. AFTER ALL, YOU'RE A *RESIDENT* OF THE THIRTEENTH FLOOR NOW, AND THEREFORE PART OF MY LITTLE CIRCLE OF FRIENDS.

AH, SO YOU MUST BE THE WITCH EVERYONE IS SO *IMPRESSED* WITH. I USED TO HAVE UNAUTHORIZED WITCHES *HANGED* IN MY EMPIRE.

AMONG SO MANY *OTHER* ACTS OF EXCESS.

ONCE AGAIN, *WHAT* DO YOU *WANT* FROM ME?

YOU WERE ATTEMPTING TO CONJURE IN YOUR ROOM LAST NIGHT. THAT SIMPLY WON'T DO. NOW THAT YOU'RE ONE OF US, YOU NEED TO *CONDUCT* YOURSELF AS SUCH.

HOW DID YOU--?

SPELLS DON'T WORK WHEN YOU'VE GOT NO POWER SOURCE TO *DRAW* FROM. AND YOU'VE NO POWER IN MY GROUP, SAVE THAT I ALLOW IT.

I'VE SEVERED ALL OF YOUR LINKS TO OUTSIDE SOURCES. LEARN TO *BEHAVE* YOURSELF.

In Tiabrut...

LOOK *OUT,* MOUSE. GOB TO YOUR REAR.

I SAW HIM.

DID YOU THINK I WASN'T *AWARE* OF HIM LURKING BACK THERE WAITING FOR HIS CHANCE TO STICK A KNIFE IN?

JUST LOOKING OUT FOR MY BEST *MATE.*

NO OFFENSE INTENDED.

YOU TEND TO *YOUR* SHARE, FREDDY, AND I'LL TEND TO MINE.

𝕋HE FARM.

THAT WAS NICE.

ONLY NICE?

OKAY, CAPTAIN SINBAD, SIR, IT WAS *WONDERFUL*-- WHICH IS, Y'KNOW, NICE.

SO, HOW WILL WE FILL THE NEXT TWENTY MINUTES, UNTIL YOU CAN--WELL, *YOU* KNOW, GO AGAIN?

YOU TELL *ME*. YOU ALWAYS HAVE AN IDEA IN MIND FOR SUCH NECESSARY PAUSES.

WELL, YOU COULD TELL ME MORE OF YOUR *ADVENTURES* AFTER THE GLORY BURNED.

WHEN YOU LAST LEFT OFF, YOU WERE GUARDING PRINCE CHARMING WHILE HE WAS PULLING THE FINAL CARPET BOMB.

OH, YES. WE'D JUST DISPATCHED THE GOBLIN PATROL. THERE WERE ONLY SIX OF THEM, AND ONLY TWO SURVIVED LONG ENOUGH TO APPROACH WITHIN RANGE OF MY SCIMITAR.

COMMANDER CHARMING FINISHED THE FOUR WITH HIS RIFLE, BUT IT WAS AN IFFY THING, WHAT WITH THE BURN INJURIES TO HIS FACE AND EYES. HIS LONG DISTANCE AIM WAS OFF.

"HE HAD TO WASTE SEVEN PRECIOUS ROUNDS TO HIT FOUR GOBS--BULLETS WE COULDN'T *AFFORD* TO SPEND."

DAMMIT!

I'VE GOT HIM.

"LATER WE *MUTUALLY* DECIDED, FABLETOWN REGULATIONS BE DAMNED, ONE OF YOUR ARABIAN ALLIES HAD TO LEARN HOW TO USE A *MODERN* WEAPON."

IT'S A BREACH LOADER, WHICH MEANS THE BULLETS GO IN HERE.

HMMM.

THERE! DID YOU **SEE** THAT? I HIT THE GOBLIN EVEN THOUGH HE WAS AT LEAST A HUNDRED YARDS AWAY! THIS IS AN AMAZING WEAPON! BETTER THAN THE GREATEST MAGIC SWORD!

CLOSER TO **SIXTY** YARDS, BUT A BLOODY GOOD SHOT FOR A FIRST-TIMER.

OF COURSE LATER I DEDUCED HIS **REAL** PLAN.

ONCE I KNEW HOW TO USE THE RIFLE, I COULD REMAIN OUT-SIDE OF THE LAST GATEWAY AND DEFEND OUR POSITION, WHILE HE WENT IN TO ACTIVATE THE BOMB.

I THINK HE KNEW ALL ALONG THAT HE'D HAVE TO SACRIFICE HIMSELF, LEAVING ME OF TWO MINDS. I WANT TO MOURN HIM, ALONG WITH THE REST OF YOU.

BUT AT THE SAME TIME, I CAN'T FEEL ANY-THING BUT **PRIDE** FOR WHAT HE DID. I IMAGINE YOUR CULTURE WOULD FIND THE JOY I FEEL IN POOR TASTE.

BUT IN MY LANDS SUCH COURAGE HAS TO BE **CELEBRATED** MORE THAN MOURNED. SO, HOW FAR DO YOU WANT ME TO TELL THIS TALE?

ALL THE WAY TO THE **END**, OF COURSE.

AH, BUT I FEAR THE NATURAL END OF MY TALE OF GRAND HEROICS IS WHEN YOU AND I FINALLY TELL BOY BLUE ABOUT OUR NEW... RELATIONSHIP.

I DON'T WANT TO **TALK** ABOUT THAT RIGHT NOW.

MAYBE WE SHOULD GET SOME SLEEP. BUSY DAY TOMORROW.

IN TIABRUT...

AREN'T YOU GOING TO HELP ME LOAD THE *WAGONS*?

FREDDY? ARE YOU *LISTENING* TO ME? WE NEED TO LOAD THE WAGONS, BURY THE LOOT SOMEWHERE SAFE, AND THEN COME BACK FOR MORE.

AND THEN DO THAT AGAIN AND AGAIN, ALL BEFORE ANYONE *ELSE* THINKS OF WANDERING UP THIS WAY.

IT OCCURS TO ME, MY FRIEND, THAT IN THIS VAST ROOM OF *AMAZING* WEALTH, THE ONE BOX THEY STILL KEPT UNDER LOCK AND KEY MIGHT CONTAIN THE *GREATEST* TREASURE OF ALL.

WELL REASONED! LET'S *OPEN* IT!

I'LL BET YOUR BATTLE AX COULD CUT THROUGH THESE OLD CHAINS WELL ENOUGH.

HRRMPH!

POSSIBLY SO.

STILL, IT WOULD LIKELY RUIN MY AX'S *BLADE,* THOUGH.

SO WHAT? COMPARED TO WHAT MIGHT BE *INSIDE* THE STONE BOX, WHAT'S ONE MEASLY *AX?*

TRUE.

BUY YOUR-SELF A THOUSAND MORE WHEN WE'RE *DONE* HERE!

HIT IT! GIVE IT A GREAT *WHACK!*

WANG!

HMMM. TOUGH CHAIN.

TRY IT AGAIN! REALLY GIVE IT A *GOOD ONE* THIS TIME!

WANG!

YOU *DID* IT! QUICK! LET'S OPEN THE BOX AND SEE THE GREATEST TREASURE OF ALL!

IN THE FORMER EMPIRE WORLD OF TIABRUT...

SO, NIMBLE MISTER MOUSE AND STALWART MISTER FREDDY CAME IN SEARCH OF TREASURE AND SPOILS.

BUT WHAT DID THEY FIND?

WELL, I'M VALUABLE ENOUGH, THOUGH IT REMAINS TO BE SEEN IF YOU'LL CONSIDER ME MUCH OF A TREASURE.

AND I'M MOST CERTAINLY NOT SPOILED, EVEN THOUGH I'VE BEEN COOPED UP IN THIS CRAMPED AND DREARY STONE BOX FOR AN AWFUL LONG TIME.

BOXES

Chapter Two of THE DARK AGES

MEANWHILE...

JUST LIKE OLD TIMES, HUH?

...IN FABLETOWN...

THE *THREE COMPADRES* ARE BACK IN ACTION, SCORING THEIR WEEKLY DOSE OF COMIC BOOKS AND CANDY.

NOW, IF WE JUST HAD A TRIO OF HOT *GIRLS*, THIS WOULD BE A PERFECT DAY.

BOOKS

HEY, I GOT AN IDEA! WHY DON'T WE HOOK UP WITH THOSE THREE *ARABIAN* HOTTIES THAT MOVED IN SINCE I WAS LAST HERE?

THEY'VE CERTAINLY GOT ALL SORTS OF *VA-VA-VOOM!* THEY'VE GOT MORE WIGGLES THAN A FLOCK OF MONGOOSES, IF YOU CATCH MY MEANING.

OR IS IT *MONGEESE?*

I CAN'T DO THAT, PINOCCHIO. RIDING HOOD SAYS I'M NOT ALLOWED TO *SPEAK* TO THEM ANYMORE. I'M NOT SURE WHY.

I'M SURE WHY.

EVEN THOUGH YOU'VE CUT OFF MY ABILITY TO CONJURE, I STILL HAVE **CONNECTIONS** IN PLACE TO MY OLD EMPIRE.

I CAN SENSE WHEN CERTAIN THINGS HAVE BEEN DISRUPTED, AND THEY HAVE. ONE OF THE **BROADCAST BOXES** HAS BEEN OPENED.

AND WHAT MIGHT THEY BE?

AH, SO YOU DON'T KNOW **EVERY-THING**, DO YOU?

THE BOXES WERE USED TO POWER MY **SORCERERS CORPS** BY BROADCASTING WHATEVER MAGICAL SOURCE WAS CONTAINED WITHIN.

ONE OR MORE PER WORLD WOULD BE ENOUGH TO SUPPLY--

WELL, SUFFICE IT TO SAY, THEY CONTAIN GREAT OLD POWERS. NOW AT LEAST **ONE** OF THOSE OLD POWERS HAS BEEN RELEASED BACK INTO THE WORLDS.

YOU **SERIOUSLY** OVERSTEPPED IN DESTROYING MY EMPIRE. BY ANY MEASURE, WE **SOLVED** MORE PROBLEMS THAN WE CREATED.

SOMETHING THAT TOOK CENTURIES AND ENTIRE ARMIES TO SAFELY LOCK AWAY IS LOOSE AGAIN AND **YOU** CAUSED IT.

I WONDER HOW LONG WE'LL BE ABLE TO SURVIVE THE RESULTS OF YOUR NOBLE **MEDDLING**.

A FEW HOURS LATER...

WHAT'S THIS?

THE WITCHING CLOAK. YOU ASKED ME TO FETCH IT.

YOU SAID DOCTOR SWINEHEART NEEDED IT DOWN AT THE INFIRMARY--SOMETHING TO DO WITH BLUE'S LATEST OPERATION.

I DID. HE DOES. BUT WHAT'S THAT IN YOUR HANDS? THOSE ARE OLD RAGS.

IT *WAS* THE CLOAK WHEN I PICKED IT UP! HONEST!

BUT THEN IT SORT OF CAME ALL APART WHEN I GRABBED IT! AND NOT ONLY THAT, I SUDDENLY HAD TO POOP REALLY BAD, AND NOW THERE'S A BIG MESS BACK IN THE--

NOT-- ANOTHER-- *WORD!*

BUFKIN, WHAT DID I *TELL* YOU ABOUT THIS? THERE ARE SOME SUBJECTS THAT ARE FIT FOR POLITE CONVERSATION AND SOME THAT *AREN'T!*

YOUR BATHROOM HABITS BELONG *STRICTLY* IN THE SECOND CATEGORY!

BUT, MISS BEAUTY, THIS WASN'T THE USUAL POOP! IT WAS ALL WET AND MESSY AND *EXPLOSIVE* EVEN! IT'S SPLATTERED EVERYWHERE!

I-- THINK IT'S OVER.

PROMISE?

HOW WOULD *I* KNOW? I'VE NEVER BEEN THROUGH AN EARTHQUAKE BEFORE. SINCE WHEN DOES NEW YORK EVEN *HAVE* THEM?

I MEANT, DO YOU PROMISE *YOU* DIDN'T CAUSE THIS BECAUSE YOU'RE MAD AT ME?

DON'T BE DAFT. I DON'T HAVE THOSE KINDS OF POWERS.

REALLY? BUT PRINCE CHARMING (MAY HE REST IN PEACE) ALWAYS *SAID* YOU DID! HE SAID YOU COULD BURN MY *HEART* OUT WITH YOUR LASER BEAM EYES!

PRINCE CHARMING ENJOYED *TORMENTING* YOU. SOMETIMES I CAN SEE WHY IT HAD ITS CHARMS.

YOU LOOK IN BACK TO SEE WHAT'S BEEN BROKEN. I'M GOING TO CHECK OUTSIDE TO SEE WHAT I CAN SEE.

AND MAKE SURE YOU CLEAN UP THAT EARLIER *MESS* YOU MENTIONED, OR I'LL *LASER BEAM* YOU FOR CERTAIN!

YES, MA'AM.

WHAT DO YOU MEAN, "NOTHING HAPPENED"? I SWEAR THE WHOLE DAMNED *BUILDING* SHOOK, NOT FIVE MINUTES AGO!

NOT OUT HERE. MAYBE YOU DREAMED IT?

THIS MAKES *NO* SENSE!

"I WASN'T DREAMING, GRIMBLE! I WASN'T EVEN ASLEEP! *YOU'RE* THE ONE WHO NAPS THE DAY AWAY!

"I *DEMAND* THAT YOU GET OFF YOUR ASS AND SEE IF ANYONE ELSE NOTICED THE EARTHQUAKE!

"YOU'RE SUPPOSED TO BE THE WOODLAND'S SECURITY OFFICER, SO *ACT* LIKE IT! CHECK TO SEE IF WE'RE SECURE!"

NOW, *THIS* IS INTERESTING.

I'M FREE AT *LAST*.

BUT THROUGH NO EFFORT OF MY OWN.

WHO, THEN, CAUSED THIS FORTUNATE TURN?

AND WHAT ADVANTAGE IS *BABA YAGA* TO MAKE OF IT?

AND JUST OUTSIDE THE WOODLAND BUILDING...

HEY, BROOME? DOES THIS COFFIN FEEL TOO LIGHT?

WELL, THERE'S NO ONE *IN* IT.

CAREFUL NOT TO *SCRAPE* IT, THOUGH. IT'S GOT TO BE PERFECT FOR THE MEMORIAL.

SO WE'RE JUST GOING TO BURY AN EMPTY BOX? SOMEHOW THAT DOESN'T SEEM--Y'KNOW-- *ENOUGH.*

NOT *ENTIRELY* EMPTY. THERE'LL BE ONE OF CHARMING'S UNIFORMS INSIDE, SOME OF HIS FAVORITE SWORDS AND A *SHIT-LOAD* OF HIS MEDALS.

UH, MISS BEAUTY? CAN WE *HELP* YOU WITH SOMETHING?

NO SHAKEN BUILDINGS? NO RUMBLING? NOTHING? YOU DIDN'T SEE OR HEAR A THING?

EXCUSE ME?

NEVER MIND. *CARRY ON!*

WHAT AN ODD WOMAN.

PRETTY, THOUGH.

TRUE. THAT MAKES UP FOR A *LOT.*

NEXT: THE GREAT UNBINDING

The Farm.

...WHILE HE LIVED, ENTIRE *WORLDS* WEREN'T ENOUGH TO CONTAIN HIM. NOW SIX GOOD FEET OF EARTH ARE SUFFICIENT.

FABLETOWN UNBOUND

Chapter Three of THE DARK AGES

HE WILL BE *DEARLY* MISSED--MY RIVAL ONCE, MY FRIEND LATER, AND OUR TRUSTED LEADER IN A TIME OF CRISIS.

IN THIS UNTIDY LITTLE CORNER OF THE UNIVERSE, WHERE SO MANY OF US WERE REPUTED TO BE "THE FAIREST IN ALL THE LAND," *NONE* OF US WAS ENTIRELY SAFE AROUND HIM.

BUT HE WAS A BETTER MAN THAN *I* EVER GAVE HIM CREDIT FOR, AND A MORE HONORABLE MAN THAN HE EVER GAVE *HIMSELF* CREDIT FOR.

HE WAS PERSONALLY BRAVE-- MOST OF THE TIME--AND A SKILLED, COURAGEOUS AND AUDACIOUS MILITARY LEADER *ALL* OF THE TIME.

I DON'T THINK I CAN BE ACCUSED OF HYPERBOLE WHEN I SAY THAT FABLETOWN CONTINUES TO *EXIST* TODAY BECAUSE HE WAS WITH US OVER THE PAST FEW YEARS.

HE WAS HERE WHEN WE *NEEDED* HIM, IN OUR MOST UNCERTAIN HOUR, AND GAVE THE LAST FULL MEASURE OF HIMSELF FOR EACH OF US.

ULTIMATELY, WHAT GREATER THING COULD BE SAID OF *ANY* MAN, LIVING *OR* DEAD?

AT THE SAME TIME, THE KNIGHTS OF MALTA HOSPITAL...

NURSE?

NURSE!

THE SECRET FABLES-ONLY CLINIC ON ITS TOP THREE FLOORS.

WHAT DO YOU *WANT,* MR. BLUE? WHAT DO YOU NEED *THIS* TIME?

CAN'T YOU SEE WE'RE UNDER-STAFFED TODAY?

EVERYONE'S UP AT THE FARM FOR THE *MEMORIAL* SERVICE.

I--

OF COURSE *I* WASN'T ALLOWED TO GO. NO, I HAD TO STAY *HERE* AND NURSEMAID YOU.

I DON'T FEEL WELL.

IT'S TO BE EXPECTED. YOU'RE RECOVERING FROM A *MAJOR* OPERATION. GETTING BETTER TAKES TIME, SO YOU CAN'T BE A *BABY* ABOUT IT.

NO, IT'S NOT MY MISSING ARM. NOT THIS TIME, IT'S--

--WHATEVER WAS HARMING MY ARM, I THINK IT'S INSIDE THE *REST* OF ME NOW. I FEEL--

NONSENSE, MR. BLUE.

DOCTOR SWINE-HEART IS A GENIUS AND A TRUE SAVANT. HE DOESN'T *MAKE* MISTAKES. IF HE SAYS YOU'LL BE FINE, THEN YOU'LL *BE* FINE.

NO MISTAKES? WHY DID IT TAKE SIX *OPERATIONS,* THEN?

AND IN A WORLD, MANY WORLDS DISTANT...

I'M SORRY, GENTLEMEN. AS MUCH AS I DEARLY *ENJOY* YOUR COMPANY, I SIMPLY CAN'T STAY LONGER.

THE SPELL OF UNBINDING IS COMPLETED AND DOING ITS WICKED WORK. TIME FOR ME TO MOVE ON TO OTHER PRIORITIES.

ONE MUSTN'T PUT OFF ONE'S VENGEANCES FOR *TOO* LONG, OR THEY BECOME STALE AND BLAND.

ABANDON YOU? NO, NOT ENTIRELY.

POP

IN A WAY I PLAN TO TAKE YOU *WITH* ME.

WHAT AM I DOING?

WHAT DO YOU *MEAN*, WHAT AM I DOING?

YOU FORGET YOURSELF, SIR. REMEMBER WHO I AM. I'M *MISTER DARK.*

AND I DO WHATEVER I WANT, *WHEN-EVER* I WANT.

AND IN THIS CASE...

...I'M EATING FREDDY'S *TEETH.*

DON'T WORRY, MOUSE.

I'LL GET TO YOU WHEN I'M DONE WITH HIM.

WHY?

OH, I SUPPOSE I COULD SAY HAVING A FEW STONY THINGS IN THE GULLET AIDS IN ONE'S *DIGES-TION.*

AND THAT MUCH WOULD BE TRUE ENOUGH. BUT YES, YOU'VE CORRECTLY GUESSED I'VE *OTHER* USES IN MIND FOR YOUR GRINDERS AS WELL.

INHUMAN? DEAR BOY, WHO-EVER SAID I WAS HUMAN?

BACK AT THE FARM...

YES, MORE AND MORE I'M CONVINCED THERE WASN'T AN *ACTUAL* EARTHQUAKE.

BUT THAT STILL MEANS SOMETHING DAMNED *ODD* HAPPENED IN THE BUSINESS OFFICE, AND I'M *DETER-MINED* TO FIND OUT *WHAT.*

YOU DO THAT, SWEETIE. TAKE YOUR *MIND* OFF--WELL--

WELL WHAT?

IT'S JUST THAT YOU WERE CRYING PRETTY *HARD* BACK THERE FOR A WHILE.

IT WAS A *FUNERAL.* I ALWAYS BAWL LIKE A LITTLE GIRL AT FUNERALS AND WEDDINGS. SO WHAT?

OKAY, IT'S JUST THAT--I MEAN HE WAS INCREDIBLY *HANDSOME* AND, WELL, HE *DID* TRY HIS LUCK WITH JUST ABOUT EVERY WOMAN IN FABLETOWN, AND--

AND SUDDENLY YOU'RE WONDERING IF I *BETRAYED* YOU?

I NEVER SLEPT WITH PRINCE CHARMING. *PERIOD!*

AND I NEVER FOR A MOMENT THOUGHT YOU DID, HONEY, ONLY--WELL, YOU *WERE* AWFUL SAD.

THE WOODLAND, THE NEXT MORNING...

ARE YOU *FEELING* OKAY, FRAU TOTENKINDER? YOU LOOK A BIT DISTRACTED.

NO, YOUNG MAN, ALL OF A SUDDEN I'M FEELING VERY MUCH *NOT* OKAY.

SOMETHING BAD IS OCCURRING.

WHERE?

HERE. ALL AROUND US.

OPEN THAT BOX *NOW!* QUICKLY!

EMPTY.

IT SURE AS HELL WASN'T THE OTHER DAY, WHEN FLY AND I WERE *CARRYING* IT. THERE WAS SOMETHING INSIDE IT-- I *SWEAR* TO IT.

YOU WEREN'T WRONG, MR. WOLF. THAT BOX CONTAINED THE BLUE FAIRY, IN HER WITHERED BUT STILL-LIVING STATE.

OVER THE PAST FEW DAYS I WAS WORKING ON SAFELY UNRAVELING THE SPELLS THAT KEPT THE BOX SHUT TIGHT FROM ANYONE BUT GEPPETTO.

BUT IT SEEMS *SOMEONE'S* BEATEN ME TO IT, AND SEVERED ALL CONNECTIONS BETWEEN THE FAIRY AND HER FORMER PRISON.

GEPPETTO.

I DOUBT IT. HE WOULDN'T WANT TO SET THE BLUE FAIRY FREE ANY MORE THAN *I* WOULD.

ELSEWHERE IN THE WOODLAND...
GOOD MORNING, GRIMBLE. NO BIG CRISES IN THE NIGHT, I TRUST?
NOPE. ALL WAS QUIET AND PEACEFUL.
GOOD. LET'S HOPE THE DAY STAYS THE SAME.
BUSINES OFFICE
HUH?
WHAT THE HELL--?

WAKE *UP*, GRIMBLE! WE'VE GOT AN *EMERGENCY!* THE BUSINESS OFFICE IS MISSING!

WHADAYA *MEAN*, MISSING?

THAT'S *GONE*, TOO?

"GONE TOO"? EXPLAIN *"GONE TOO!"*

BIGBY AND I WERE JUST UP IN BLUEBEARD'S OLD APARTMENT. BUT HIS CASTLE IS NO LONGER *INSIDE* OF IT. THERE'S JUST A NORMAL *UNOCCUPIED* APARTMENT THERE NOW.

AND THERE'S JUST A NORMAL *CUBBYHOLE*-SIZED OFFICE WHERE THE BUSINESS OFFICE USED TO BE!

BECAUSE THE SPELLS BINDING THEM BOTH TO THE WOODLAND BUILDING HAVE BEEN *CANCELLED.*

MEANING *WHAT,* EXACTLY? THEY NO LONGER EXIST?

OF *COURSE* THEY STILL EXIST. BOTH PLACES WERE NEVER ACTUALLY HERE, BUT THEY WERE *TIED* TO THE WOODLAND BY STRONG ENCHANTMENTS.

EVACUATE THE HOSPITAL? THAT'S A *RIDICULOUS* NOTION! WHY WOULD I CONSIDER DOING THAT?

AND WHERE WOULD WE *GO*? WHERE COULD WE TRANSFER MY *PATIENTS*?

THE FARM? ARE YOU ENTIRELY *INSANE*, WOMAN? IT'S A DAY'S DRIVE AWAY AND I HAVE TOO MUCH PRECIOUS *EQUIPMENT* TO TRANSPORT.

HAS SOMEONE PUT YOU UP TO PLAYING A PRACTICAL JOKE ON ME? I WARN YOU NOW, I FIND SUCH THINGS HIGHLY *IMPRACTICAL* INDEED!

...OF ALL THE RIDICULOUS BUREAUCRATIC *BLUNDERS*!

DOCTOR SWINEHEART? IS SOMETHING *TROUBLING* YOU?

NOT *NOW*, NURSE SPRAT! GO FIND A PATIENT WHO NEEDS CARE!

GOOD NEWS, MR. BLUE. DID YOU MENTION YOU MISSED THE FARM?

WELL, WE'VE DECIDED TO SEND YOU *UP* THERE THIS AFTERNOON.

ARE YOU SURE I'M WELL ENOUGH TO BE DISCHARGED?

I DON'T KNOW IF THE NURSE TOLD YOU, BUT I DON'T *FEEL* VERY GOOD.

WE'LL FIX THAT, STARTING WITH A LARGE DOSE OF FRESH AIR. DO *WONDERS* FOR YOU.

NOW WHAT?

NOW I GUESS WE WAIT TO SEE WHAT HAPPENS.

YOU *KNOW* THIS HAS TO BE A FALSE ALARM. THESE BUILDINGS ARE SOLID.

EXCEPT THAT WE FORTIFIED EACH ONE OF THEM WITH STRONG ENCHANTMENTS. THAT MIGHT TURN OUT TO BE SHORT-SIGHTED OF US.

I *WARNED* YOU SOMETHING LIKE THIS MIGHT HAPPEN.

NOW, POPS, *FESS UP.* NO, YOU DIDN'T. OR AT LEAST NOT SOON ENOUGH TO *DO* ANYTHING ABOUT IT. IT WAS MORE OF AN "I TOLD YOU SO," WASN'T IT?

WHEN CAN WE GO BACK IN?

GOOD QUESTION.

NEXT: OUR DARKEST HOUR

TWO MINUTES AFTER THE WOODLAND BUILDING CAME CRASHING DOWN.

OKAY, I *KNOW* YOU PEOPLE ARE OUT THERE.

I CAN *HEAR* YOU.

GRIMBLE! WHAT ARE YOU *DOING?* WE NEED TO MOVE THESE PEOPLE *OUT* OF HERE!

BIGBY! MOVE WHO *WHERE?* I CAN'T SEE A DAMNED THING IN THIS DUST CLOUD.

AND I CAN'T CATCH MY BREATH! I KEEP SPITTING OUT DIRT. I THINK ALL THIS GRIT'S GETTING INTO MY LUNGS.

COUGH! COUGH! COUGH!

HANG IN THERE, BUDDY. I THINK THIS IS A SITUATION WHERE MY SPECIAL *TALENTS* CAN HELP.

COUGH! COUGH!

THUMP THUMP

BETTER KEEP MOVING. TRY TO CONTACT AS MANY PEOPLE AS YOU CAN BUMP INTO.

TELL THEM TO HUNKER DOWN.

IT'S ABOUT TO GET *WINDY.*

GET *DOWN,* PEOPLE! GRAB THE PAVEMENT AND COVER YOUR *HEADS!*

BIGBY'S GOING TO *BLOW* THE DUST AWAY!

OH, PINOCCHIO, YOU AND YOUR DAD NEED TO DUCK AND COVER. BIGBY'S GOING TO--

YES, I *HEARD* YOU *SHOUTING.* BUT I'M NOT ABOUT TO GET ON MY KNEES, OUT IN THE STREET, LIKE SOME CRINGING, PENNILESS *BEGGAR.*

SUIT YOURSELF, OLD-TIMER. HOPE YOU LAND SOMEWHERE *SOFT.*

C'MON, POPS. WE NEED TO *DO* THIS. I'VE BEEN CLOSE TO BIGBY WHEN HE HUFFS AND PUFFS BEFORE. YOU DON'T WANT TO TAKE UP *FLYING LESSONS* NOW, DO YOU?

OH, NO YOU DON'T, SIR! *NO YOU DON'T!*

YOU DON'T GET TO SINK INTO DESPAIR! YOU'RE OUR *MAYOR*--OUR LEADER! AND NOW IT'S TIME TO STEP UP AND *LEAD!*

WITH ALL DUE RESPECT, KING COLE, WE DIDN'T ELECT YOU TO ENJOY THE PRIVILEGES OF OFFICE WHEN TIMES ARE *GOOD*, BUT TO SHOULDER THE HEAVIEST WEIGHT IN THE *BAD* TIMES!

WELL, TIMES ARE SURE BAD *NOW*, SO WHAT ARE YOU GOING TO *DO* ABOUT IT, SIR?'

I DON'T-- I'M NOT SURE WHAT--

PLEASE MOVE THESE FOLKS OUT OF THE WAY, MR. GRANDOURS. I NEED TO SPEAK TO THE MAYOR.

I THINK YOU NEED TO MAKE YOURSELF *SCARCE*, BIGBY.

THE MUNDY EMERGENCY RESPONSE PEOPLE WILL BE HERE SOO IN FULL FORCE, AND THEY CAN FIND A GIANT *WOLF* WHEN THEY ARRIVE.

BETTER CHANGE BACK.

FINE ENOUGH, BUT GET READY TO SEE ME *STARKERS*, THEN, BEAUTY. MY CLOTHES BLEW AWAY SOME- WHERE.

:COUGH! COUGH!:

:COUGH! COUGH!:

:COUGH! COUGH!:

THIS ISN'T AS BAD AS IT'S GOING TO *GET,* MR. MAYOR. WHATEVER CAUSED THIS IS ON ITS WAY HERE NOW. I CAN FEEL HIM COMING CLOSER WITH EVERY HEARTBEAT.

WHO *IS* IT? WHO COULD'VE *DONE* THIS TO US?

I DON'T KNOW.

I CAN'T GET MUCH OF A SENSE OF HIM, EXCEPT THAT HE'S A DESTROYER, HE'S MORE POWERFUL THAN WE CAN HANDLE. *AND* HE'S ON HIS WAY.

WE NEED TO LEAVE.

LEAVE? WHERE?

THIS IS THE *TIME,* SIR.

LEAD US. WE'RE ALL WAITING TO FOLLOW YOU.

UHM... WELL...

...WHAT ABOUT THE *FARM?* HAS THAT BEEN HARMED, TOO?

NOT A BIT. EVERY SPELL THERE IS STILL INTACT. WE'VE NO REASON TO BELIEVE THE FARM ISN'T HIDDEN FROM MUNDY AND UNKNOWN ENEMY ALIKE.

THEN THAT'S WHAT WE HAVE TO DO. *THAT'S* WHERE WE'LL GO.

THE FARM.

HOURS LATER...

ROSE RED?

YOU *HAVE* TO WAKE UP, ROSE RED. THERE'S *TROUBLE*.

WHO--?

COME DOWN-STAIRS.

WHO *IS* THIS? I DON'T RECOGNIZE--

HURRY. I DON'T HAVE MUCH TIME.

WHAT THE FUCK--?!!

I THOUGHT I WAS ALL DONE, BUT THEY SENT ME BACK.

DO YOU *REMEMBER* ME, ROSE RED? MY NAME WAS COLIN. I USED TO *LIVE* HERE AT THE FARM.

YOU'RE A BLOODY *PIG HEAD* ON A *STICK!*

AND YOU'RE *DEAD!* I SAW YOU DIE!

OF *COURSE* I'M DEAD. I'D HATE TO BE IN THIS CONDITION AND *NOT* BE.

NOW, YOU'RE GOING TO HAVE TO *CALM DOWN*, BECAUSE THEY NEVER GIVE ME MUCH TIME.

I USED TO VISIT YOUR *SISTER* LIKE THIS, BACK WHEN THINGS WERE BAD AND IT WAS ALL GOING TO LAND ON *HER* SHOULDERS.

BUT NOW IT FALLS ON *YOU.*

EVERYTHING. ALL THE WEIGHT.

AND IT'S MY TASK TO *WARN* YOU--TO GIVE YOU TIME TO SUMMON UP THE STRENGTH TO FACE WHAT'S COMING.

WARN ME ABOUT *WHAT?* WHAT THE HELL ARE YOU TALKING ABOUT?

THE BAD TIMES ARE BACK-- PERHAPS WORSE THAN EVER. DON'T YOU SEE? THERE WAS *ALWAYS* GOING TO BE A PRICE FOR THE WITCHING CLOAK, AND THE WELL, AND THINGS LIKE THAT.

YOU HAD THEM FOR *CENTURIES*, TO USE AS YOU WOULD, BUT NOW THE BILL'S COME DUE.

AND SOON, WHEN THE *DUST* SETTLES, THEY'LL BE LOOK- ING TO YOU, TO *GUIDE* THEM THROUGH THE DARKNESS.

CAN YOU *DO* IT? CAN YOU BE THEIR *LIGHT?* I CAN'T ASK SNOW AGAIN, BECAUSE SHE'S DONE. SHE'S ON A DIFFERENT PATH NOW, AND HER BURDEN HAS PASSED ON TO YOU.

GOD-*DAMMIT* ALL TO VARIOUS ROTTING HELLS!

CAN YOU *PLEASE* STOP TALKING IN VAGUE RIDDLES AND MAKE SOME *SENSE?*

I HAVE TO SAY, YOUR SISTER TREATED ME NICER.

FINE! I'LL TREAT YOU LIKE THE DAINTY GODDAMN *QUEEN* OF DAINTY GODDAMN *ENGLAND!* NOW, IF YOU'D JUST--

SORRY. I'M OUT OF TIME.

I'LL TRY TO COME BACK WHEN I CAN.

IF THEY LET ME.

WAIT!

YOU NEVER EXPLAINED ANYTHING.

SINBAD, GET UP. YOU HAVE TO GET DRESSED.

≈NRRRMPH?≈

UP *NOW!* JOIN ME DOWN-STAIRS!

SOMEWHERE IN THE ENDLESS UNIVERSE, MISTER DARK RIDES HIS WILD BLACK STEED NAMED HARBINGER, WHOSE STRIDE CROSSES WORLDS.

EVER CLOSER HE COMES TO HIS DESTINATION, AND THESE ARE THE SIGNS THAT PRESAGE HIS COMING...

IN FABLETOWN'S LOST BUSINESS OFFICE, THE WICKED WITCH BABA YAGA IS UNBOUND AND PROWLING THE BACK CORRIDORS. TENDING TO OLD HUNGERS IS FOREMOST ON HER MIND.

ON ONE OF THE OFFICE'S SECURE STORAGE SHELVES, A BOTTLE HAS COME OPEN AND ITS PREVIOUS OCCUPANT IS NOWHERE TO BE FOUND.

AND AT THE NORTH POLE...

PAPA, WHAT'S WRONG?

I WAS WORKING ON THE NAUGHTY AND NICE LISTS, MAMA, AND *LOOK!*

THE NAUGHTY LIST IS GROWING OUT OF CONTROL. ALL OF THESE CHILDREN SUDDENLY WAKING UP TO THE USUALLY DORMANT KERNELS OF *EVIL* THAT SLEEP INSIDE ALL OF US.

I'VE BEEN WRITING FOR HOURS AND *STILL* THE NAMES ARE COMING TO ME.

AND IN THEIR SLUMBERS THE WORLD OVER, CHILDREN WAKE IN THE NIGHT, KNOWING THAT SOMETHING IS ABOUT TO COME CRAWLING OUT FROM UNDER THE BED.

MR. BOGEY MAN?

OH NO, *THAT* WON'T DO. DOCTOR SWINEHEART NEEDS TO *SET UP* IN THAT ROOM FOR BOY BLUE. THEY'RE BRINGING HIS VAN UP TO OFFLOAD BLUE NOW. *HE* COMES FIRST.

EXCUSE ME? WHY WOULD BLUE NEED "OFF-LOADING"?

WHAT'S THAT, DEAR? UH--HOLD ON--OH, *NO* YOU DON'T! YOU AREN'T LEAVING THAT HERE! PUT THAT BACK IN YOUR *TRUCK* AND TAKE IT OVER TO--

OH, THAT'S RIGHT, MISS RED. YOU WON'T HAVE HEARD. BOY BLUE WAS TAKEN *ILL* AGAIN. THAT'S HIS TRANSPORT COMING UP NOW. YOU CAN TALK TO HIM, IF YOU LIKE.

NO DOUBT HE COULD USE A FRIENDLY VOICE RIGHT NOW.

BLUE?

BUT HE WAS *FINE.*

STAND BACK PLEASE, MISS. WE NEED TO UNLOAD A STRETCHER HERE.

OH, DEAR GOD, BLUE, WHAT *HAPPENED?*

HELLO, ROSE. THEY TELL ME I'LL BE BUNKING UP HERE AGAIN. JUST LIKE *OLD* TIMES, HUH?

YOU CAN TALK TO GIRLS *LATER*, YOUNG MAN. THE DOCTOR WANTS YOU INSIDE AND OUT OF THIS CHILL AIR *ASAP.*

I'D SHAKE YOUR HAND, BUT THE ONLY ONE LEFT IS FULL OF *TUBES* JUST NOW.

IF YOU TWO DON'T *MIND*, I THINK I'D BETTER BE TAKEN INSIDE NOW.

NURSE?

BIGBY, THIS CAN'T HAPPEN--NOT TO HIM. WE *CAN'T* LOSE THE BOY. WHAT HAVEN'T WE *TRIED* YET?

THE DOCTOR IS OUT OF IDEAS. TOTENKINDER AND THE OTHER SORCERERS SAY THERE'S NOTHING LEFT *THEY* CAN TRY, EITHER.

I THINK OUR BEST BET IS WITH FLYCATCHER, WHENEVER HE SHOWS UP AGAIN. HE'S PRETTY POWERFUL NOW. MAYBE *HE* HAS A LAST MIRACLE UP HIS SLEEVE.

BUT, WITHOUT ACCESS TO THE BUSINESS OFFICE AND THE WITCHING CLOAK, WE'VE NO *QUICK* WAY TO CONTACT HIM.

NEXT: ONE LAST MIRACLE

NEW YORK CITY.

THE TRUTH IS, CAPTAIN, I HAVEN'T THE SLIGHTEST *IDEA* WHAT HAPPENED HERE.

BULLFINCH STREET (FORMERLY FABLETOWN).

WELL, ANYONE CAN SEE *WHAT* HAPPENED, BUT WHAT I MEAN IS, BARRING FURTHER INVESTIGATION, I DON'T HAVE A *CLUE* AS TO THE CAUSE.

I'D QUESTION THE SURVIVORS, BUT THERE *AREN'T* ANY-- AND NO BODIES, EITHER.

AT LEAST NONE THAT WE'VE LOCATED SO FAR. PLACE SEEMS DESERTED. WE'LL BE A WEEK AT *LEAST* SEARCHING THE RUBBLE TO MAKE SURE.

WELL, THIS DIDN'T JUST *HAPPEN*, LIEUTENANT. NATURAL DISASTERS DON'T CONFINE THEMSELVES TO ONE SMALL CITY BLOCK.

THE BLUE HORI-ZON

Chapter five of THE DARK AGES

SO **LEAVE** NOW AND NEVER COME BACK. FORGET THIS PLACE FOR ALL TIME.

THIS IS MY **COMMAND** TO YOU AND ALL LIKE YOU.

THE STREET BELONGS TO **ME** NOW.

Y-YES SSSIR.

ASSS YOU C-COMMAND.

THAT'S IT. MOVE ALONG SMARTLY, LITTLE **MAYFLIES,** LEST YOU INCUR YOUR OWN **SCOLDINGS.**

THIS SMALL CORNER OF YOUR CITY NO LONGER **EXISTS** FOR ANY OF YOU.

AND NOW-- :ACHT-PHUUU!:

--ONE TOOTH EACH FROM FREDDY AND MOUSE.

SPAT UP TO WORK MY DESIRE.

WHO CALLS US BACK FROM BEYOND THE VEIL--

--THROUGH WHICH WE'RE NOT GIVEN TO PASS ON OUR OWN?

YOUR *MASTER* CALLS YOU, AND THAT'S ALL YOU NEED TO KNOW.

THIRTY-TWO TIMES I'LL BE ABLE TO SUMMON YOU TO DO MY WILL.

WELL, *SLIGHTLY* LESS OFTEN FOR YOU, FREDDY, BECAUSE YOU DIDN'T TAKE QUITE THE DEVOTED CARE OF YOUR *TEETH* THAT YOUR FRIEND MOUSE DID.

YOUR FIRST TASK IS TO SEARCH WHAT REMAINS OF THESE NEW RUINS.

FIND ME ONE OF THE SO-CALLED *FABLES* WHO SO RECENTLY DWELLED HERE-- IF ANY STILL REMAIN.

THE FARM.

WHERE *IS* HE? WHERE'S *BLUE?*

FLYCATCHER!

UH...I MEAN, *KING AMBROSE!* THANK *GOD* YOU'RE HERE!

I CAME AS SOON AS I HEARD! *TAKE* ME TO HIM!

THAT NIGHT...

WHAT COULD BE TAKING SO LONG? FLY'S BEEN IN THERE WITH BLUE FOR *HOURS!*

I GUESS IT TAKES AS LONG AS IT *TAKES*, SWEETIE.

OUR SPELLS SURROUNDING THE FARM ARE STILL STRONG. WE MAY BE SAFE HERE FOR A TIME.

I DON'T UNDERSTAND, FRAU TOTENKINDER. WHAT COULD BE SO FRIGHTFUL THAT IT'S GOT *YOU* SCARED?

YOU WERE ALWAYS THE TYPE TO TAKE ON ALL HELL WITH NOTHING BUT A BUCKET OF WATER.

LIKE MOST PEOPLE, CHILD, I SUPPOSE I FEAR WHAT I CAN'T UNDERSTAND OR COMPREHEND. AND THERE'S PRECIOUS *LITTLE* THAT I CAN'T COMPREHEND.

BUT THIS THING-- IT'S A DARKNESS TO ME. I CAN SENSE SOME ASPECTS OF IT, BUT ONLY IN A VAGUE AND UNDEFINED WAY. I DO FEEL ITS POWER, AND I *KNOW* IT DESIRES OUR HARM.

I THINK IT WANTS TO REDRESS SOME WRONG WE DID IT, BUT SO HELP ME, I CAN'T PIN DOWN WHAT THAT MIGHT POSSIBLY *BE.*

ROSE RED, YOU HAVE TO GET UP.

AND IT'S TERRIBLY *CLOSE.* RIGHT NOW IT'S BUBBLING AND BOILING DOWN IN FABLE- TOWN. IF WE WERE THERE, WE'D *ALL* BE DESTROYED BY NOW.

HOURS PASS.

I'M SORRY.

I FAILED.

TRY AS I MAY, I COULDN'T DO ANYTHING FOR BLUE.

ONE OR TWO AT A TIME, WE ALL NEED TO SAY OUR GOODBYES NOW.

I'VE STRENGTHENED HIM AS MUCH AS I CAN, BUT HE WON'T *LAST* MUCH LONGER.

I'M GOING FIRST, AND THERE BETTER NOT BE *ANY* ARGUMENTS ABOUT THAT!

HANG THERE A MINUTE, DAD, WHILE I--

HEY, WHERE'D MY DAD GET OFF TO?

ELSEWHERE ON THE FARM...

GOOD TREES.

NOT MUCH *MAGIC* IN THEM, THOUGH.

ON BULLFINCH STREET.

NOW THERE ARE THREE OF YOU, MY WITHERLINGS.

AND SOON THERE WILL BE MORE TO COME, EVEN IF I HAVE TO *SCULPT* THEM FROM THE DULL CLAY OF MORTALS.

AND AS IT LOOKS AS THOUGH I MAY BE HERE AWHILE, I NEED A PLACE TO *LIVE*-- A PALACE *FIT* FOR ME. *CASTLE DARK.*

YES, SIR.

BUILD IT *HERE,* OUT OF THE RUBBLE AND REMAINS OF ALL THE STRUCTURES ON THIS STREET.

AND BUILD IT *LARGE*--EACH ROOM A GLORIOUS *CHAMBER.*

I'VE HAD QUITE ENOUGH OF SMALL, ENCLOSED *BOXES.*

AS YOU WISH.

WORK NIGHT AND DAY, WITHOUT PAUSE, UNTIL YOU *FADE.*

THEN I'LL SPIT UP *ANOTHER* OF YOUR TEETH AND YOU'LL TAKE UP YOUR LABORS AGAIN.

THE FARM.

BLUE CAN'T LAST MUCH LONGER, ROSE.

AND EVERYONE'S HAD THEIR CHANCE TO SAY GOODBYE TO HIM.

EVERYONE BUT *YOU.*

WE'RE HOLDING THE ROOM FOR YOU.

LEAVE ME *ALONE!*

CAN'T YOU *SEE* I'M SICK?

I'LL GO SEE HIM WHEN I'M WELL! I PROMISE!

BY THEN IT WILL BE TOO *LATE.*

HE WAS IN *LOVE* WITH YOU AND YOU SHOULD AT LEAST--

LISTEN CLOSE, YOU INSUFFERABLE LITTLE *BRAT.* GET UP *NOW* AND GO SEE BLUE. DON'T LIE THERE ANOTHER SECOND.

IF YOU DON'T GET TO IT, THEN LEAVE THE FARM NOW AND I'LL NEVER LET SNOW OR ANY OF OUR CHILDREN SEE YOU AGAIN. YOU WOULDN'T *ENJOY* THE CONSEQUENCES.

BLUE?

IT'S ME.

ROSE RED.

I'M SORRY I DIDN'T COME SOONER, BUT--

AND I UNDERSTAND IF YOU DON'T WANT TO SEE ME.

COME IN, ROSE.

OF COURSE YOU'RE WELCOME HERE, ALWAYS.

SIT DOWN. YOU LOOK EXHAUSTED.

OH, BLUE, WHAT *HAPPENED?* HOW CAN YOU BE--?

YOU WERE *SAFE.* THE WAR ENDED AND YOU WERE FINE. THIS ISN'T FAIR.

I'M AFRAID YOU'RE WRONG, ROSE. I *WAS* KILLED IN THE WAR.

LIKE SO MANY OTHERS.

TOO MANY.

JUST TOOK A BIT LONGER WITH ME.

LATE AGAIN. STORY OF MY LIFE.

HOW'S YOUR HUSBAND?

THAT'S OVER. WE--

IT WAS A MISTAKE. JUST ANOTHER STUPID *IMPULSE* OF MINE THAT--

ANYWAY, WE ENDED IT.

I DID.

OH?

I THINK, WHEN YOU SPOKE TO ME BEFORE GOING AWAY-- WHEN YOU TOLD ME HOW YOU FELT--

WELL, I THINK THAT SCARED ME, BECAUSE WE WERE SUCH GOOD FRIENDS, AND I DIDN'T WANT TO *LOSE* THAT. OR MAYBE I THOUGHT--

NEW YORK, NEW YORK.

THE TRAIL ENDS HERE.

GONE COLD.

BUT THEY'LL RETURN AGAIN. I SENSE IT.

IN ONES, OR TWOS, OR IN GROUPS LARGE OR SMALL, THEY'LL COME BACK HERE SOMEDAY AND FIND ME WAITING FOR THEM.

TIME IS NOTHING TO ME. I'M PATIENT TO BIDE HERE IN CASTLE DARK.

SOONER OR LATER I'LL HAVE THEM. I'LL HAVE ALL OF THEIR WONDERFUL, TASTY TEETH.

YES I WILL.

DO YOUR WORK WELL, MY WITHERLINGS. I MUST HAVE THE FINEST HALL TO RECEIVE THEM AND TO DWELL IN WHILE I RESIDE IN THIS WORLD-- SOWING MY FEARS HERE AND THERE.

GRADUALLY REMAKING THIS CITY, THIS LAND, AND THEN THIS WORLD THAT THEY LOVE INTO A THING ALL MY OWN.

UNTIL THE PLACE ENTIRE IS A FITTING REFLECTION OF ME.

NEXT: WAITING FOR THE BLUES

THE FARM.

THAT WAS A LOVELY SERVICE.

IT WAS. FLYCATCHER SPOKE WELL, AND PINOCCHIO WAS ON HIS BEST BEHAVIOR. GOOD SERVICE INDEED, BUT A *DREARY* WAY TO SPEND OUR ANNIVERSARY.

OH, IS IT--? I GUESS IT IS.

I FORGOT.

DON'T WORRY. TODAY OF *ALL* DAYS YOU HAVE A GOOD EXCUSE FOR FORGETTING. AND *ANY* SORT OF CELEBRATION WOULD BE INAPPROPRIATE.

SO INSTEAD, I GUESS I SHOULD JUST ASK YOU THE TRADITIONAL *QUESTION.*

HOW ABOUT IT, BEAUTY?

CARE TO TAKE ONE MORE CIRCLE AROUND THE SUN TOGETHER?

WITHOUT QUESTION. AND I THINK--

--HUH--?

WAITING FOR THE BLUES
(An Epilogue of Sorts for The Dark Ages)

SNOW, WE SHOULD THINK ABOUT PARKING THE CUBS WITH THEIR *GRANDFATHER* UNTIL WE KNOW JUST HOW MUCH *DANGER* WE MIGHT BE IN AT THE FARM.

WHAT DANGER, PAPA?

MORE DANGEROUS THAN GRAMPA'S CASTLE?

GRAMPAW'S CASTLE ISN'T DANGEROUS NO *MORE*, STUPID. NOT NOW THAT OUR UNCLE MONSTERS ARE GONE.

BUT IS *ANYWHERE* SAFE? UNCLE BLUE GO KILLED DEAD RIGHT HERE.

NO, I WANT TO BE LEFT ALONE.

COMPLETELY ALONE.

EITHER YOUR FATHER'S KEEP, OR HAVEN.

SOMEWHERE *SAFE*.

PERHAPS OUR POPULARITY WITH THE MUNDYS *DOES* MAKE US STRONG. BUT IF THAT'S TRUE, WHAT'S THE MECHANISM?

THAT'S JUST THE THING! WHAT IF THIS ISN'T REALLY A MUNDY WORLD? WHAT IF IT'S AS MAGICAL AS ALL THE OTHERS? *MORE* MAGICAL, EVEN, BUT IN A DIFFERENT WAY.

THIS IS A WORLD OF *STORY MAKERS*. THEY TELL TALES ABOUT US HERE, UNLIKE IN ANY OTHER WORLD. WHY?

COULD A VERY SPECIFIC TYPE OF MAGIC BE AT WORK IN *THIS* WORLD OF ALL WORLDS?

I CAN SEE YOU'VE PUT SOME *THOUGHT* INTO THIS, LITTLE BADGER. YOU'VE IMPRESSED ME.

SO, IF WE'VE A SPECIAL CONNECTION TO OUR STORIES IN THIS WORLD, DID *WE* CREATE THE STORIES AND THOSE WHO'VE WRITTEN THEM?

OR DID THE STORIES CREATE *US*?

WELL, IN MOST CASES THE STORIES CAME ALONG LONG AFTER WE WERE *ALIVE*, RIGHT? SO--

AH, BUT YOU'RE MAKING THE MISTAKE OF CHRONOLOGICAL *CAUSE AND EFFECT,* WHICH IS ESSENTIAL TO SCIENCE, BUT NOT ALWAYS TO MAGIC.

CHRONOLOGY AND MAGIC DON'T ALWAYS MIX.

MAYBE THERE'S SOME SORT OF SEPARATE *MASTER STORYTELLER.* Y'KNOW, ONE WHO CREATED BOTH US *AND* THE TALES ABOUT US.

MY WORD!

SUCH AN INTUITIVE *LEAP!* HAVE YOU EVER CONSIDERED STUDYING THE CRAFT WITH ONE OF US FROM THE 13TH FLOOR?

OH, SO *THAT'S* HOW IT'S GOING TO BE?

FINE! MOCK ME! *BELITTLE* MY IDEAS! EVERYONE *ELSE* DOES!

BUT--

WE DIDN'T--WE WEREN'T--

OF COURSE I *CAN'T* BE RIGHT, BECAUSE I'M JUST A FUNNY LITTLE WOODLAND CREATURE!

I'M ALLOWED TO MIX WITH THE IMPORTANT *HUMAN* FABLES FOR EXACTLY THE SAME REASONS THAT KINGS KEEP JESTERS.

I ONLY THINK WE SHOULD *TALK* ABOUT IT.

NO! NO MORE *TALKING*. NO MORE GODDAMN INCESSANT TALKING! I'VE HAD MY *FILL* OF IT TODAY.

DON'T YOU REALIZE IT YET? YOU WERE THE *REBOUND* GUY.

THE SOLE *PURPOSE* OF THE REBOUND GUY IS TO RECOGNIZE WHEN IT'S OVER AND NOBLY GO AWAY, WITHOUT ANY FUSS.

WE'RE *DIVORCED*. I DIVORCED YOU. ACCEPT IT AND GO AWAY.

I'M NOT GOING TO BE INVOLVED WITH ANYONE EVER AGAIN, UNTIL *BLUE* COMES BACK.

WHEN HE RETURNS I'M GOING TO SPEND AS LONG AS IT TAKES MAKING IT UP TO HIM--

--BECOMING *WORTHY* OF HIM.

OF COURSE HE'LL COME BACK, FLY. HE *HAS* TO, RIGHT? HE'S TOO *IMPORTANT* TO STAY DEAD.

I DON'T KNOW, PINOCCHIO. HE WAS ONLY EVER IN THAT ONE SMALL STORY.

NOT EVEN A *REAL* STORY.

JUST A *SILLY* LITTLE RHYME.

AND WILL SOMEONE *PLEASE* EXPLAIN TO ME HOW THAT MAKES ANY *SENSE?* BLUE WAS A GIANT, SWASHBUCKLING *SUPERHERO!*

HOW DID ALL OF THAT ESCAPE AN ENTIRE *WORLD* OF SO-CALLED WRITERS?

WHAT THE HELL WERE THEY *DOING,* WRITING SO MUCH ABOUT YOU AND ME AND EVERY OTHER DUMBSHIT FABLE WHO NEVER DID *ANYTHING* IMPORTANT?

BUT HARDLY EVEN A *WORD* ABOUT BLUE?

WHERE'S THE *JUSTICE* IN *THAT?*

HEY! I JUST HAD AN IDEA!

LET'S YOU AND ME GO OUT INTO THE MUNDY AND TRACK DOWN ALL OF THESE SHIT-FOR-BRAINS, PUSS-BUCKET *WRITERS*!

THE REAL POPULAR ONES-- ALL THOSE *BEST-SELLER* GUYS, RIGHT?

AND WE'LL HIRE THEM TO WRITE UP BLUE'S *REAL* STORIES!

WITH WHAT MONEY?

OH.

YEAH.

OKAY, *SCREW* THE MONEY. WE'LL KICK THEIR PANSY LITTLE ASSES, AND *KEEP* KICKING THEM UNTIL THEY DO WHAT WE *TELL* THEM.

AND THEN, WHEN ALL OF THESE TRUE BOOKS ABOUT BLUE COME OUT, AND THE MUNDY SCUM READ THEM, THEN BLUE WILL *HAVE* TO COME BACK!

IT'S *FOOL-PROOF*!

PINOCCHIO....

I DON'T THINK-- I THINK WE BOTH NEED TO ACCEPT THAT BLUE IS GONE.

AND NOT COMING BACK.

YOU TAKE THAT *BACK,* YOU TRAITOROUS, FLY-MUNCHING MOTHER-FUCKER!

HE WAS OUR *FRIEND!* PINOCCHIO, FLY AND BLUE--THE THREE COMPADRES!

YES, HE WAS OUR FRIEND. AND HE WAS GOOD AND HEROIC AND *ALL* OF THOSE THINGS YOU MENTIONED.

SO, WHY WOULD WE WANT TO DRAG HIM BACK INTO *THIS* WORLD OF WOES AND HEARTBREAK?

ONE THING I'VE LEARNED RECENTLY IS THAT THERE ARE, IN FACT, OTHER LIVES POSSIBLE AFTER THIS ONE. PLACES OF REWARD AND REST.

DON'T YOU THINK HE'S *EARNED* A BETTER LIFE SOMEWHERE?

CRAP.

ISN'T THIS JUST *TYPICAL?*

BAD ENOUGH THAT IT ALWAYS SEEMS TO END UP BEING A *HUMAN* FABLE WHO'S THE ONLY ONE QUALIFIED TO RUN THE FARM!

BUT NOW THAT ALL OF THE FABLETOWNERS HAD TO TUCK TAIL AND *RUN,* AFTER THEY'VE LOST THEIR *OWN* HOMES, THEY MOVE IN AND START RUNNING THINGS *HERE* TOO!

IS A SINGLE RACCOON, OR SQUIRREL, OR HEDGEHOG WELCOME AT ANY OF *THEIR* IMPORTANT MEETINGS, TO DECIDE *OUR* FUTURE? NO, OF *COURSE* NOT!

SINCE WE'RE SMALL AND FURRY-- OR FEATHERED--THEY TREAT US LIKE NEWBORN *BABIES* WHO NEED TO BE LOOKED AFTER--

--AND *TOLD* WHAT TO DO!

STOP THIS TALK RIGHT *NOW!*

YOW!

≈GULP!≈

THERE'LL BE NO MORE INSURRECTIONS WHILE *I'M* IN CHARGE OF FARM SECURITY.

OH, *REALLY?* YOU'RE IN *CHARGE,* HUH?

SO, WHEN BEAST AND GRIMBLE HAD THEIR FARM SECURITY MEETING YESTERDAY, *YOU* WERE INCLUDED IN THAT, WERE YOU?

UHM... WELL...

I'VE TAKEN DOWN EVERYONE'S NAME AND I'M READY TO TESTIFY *AGAINST* ALL OF THEM, IF ONLY YOU LET ME OFF, OR AT LEAST DON'T *COOK* ME WITHOUT A TRIAL!

CHICKEN LITTLE, DO *PLEASE* SHUT UP.

AND, CLARA? YOU'VE *NOTHING* TO WORRY ABOUT HERE. THIS ISN'T A REVOLUTIONARY MEETING OF ANY STRIPE.

THEN WHAT IS IT, STINKY?

IT'S MORE LIKE OUR OWN SMALL INFORMAL *WAKE.* WE WERE SHARING OUR MEMORIES OF BLUE AND GOT A BIT OFF TRACK.

YOU CAN SEE HOW LOSING BLUE HAS US A BIT *FRUSTRATED.* AND FRUSTRATED FOLKS WILL GRIPE. THAT'S NOT INSURRECTION, IT'S *HUMAN NATURE.* AND THE NATURE OF THE BEAST.

BUT WE NEEDN'T PISS AND MOAN ABOUT HOW UNFAIR THINGS ARE HERE AT THE FARM, BECAUSE THEY'RE ABOUT TO GET *BETTER.*

I NEED TO HEAD BACK. KING COLE WANTS TO TALK TO ME ABOUT HOUSING SOME OF THE FABLETOWN FOLKS IN HAVEN.

COMING WITH?

NO, I NEED TO GO FIND MY DAD.

HE SKIPPED BLUE'S FUNERAL-- WHICH IS *FINE*, SINCE I DOUBT HE WOULD'VE BEEN WELCOME THERE. BUT I SHOULD STILL FIND OUT WHERE HE WANDERED OFF TO.

THE "POWERS THAT BE" ARE *PARANOID* THAT HE MIGHT RUN OFF TO START NEW EMPIRES SOMEWHERE.

STUPID, THOUGH. WITHOUT THE WOODEN SOLDIERS HE'S JUST ANOTHER MEAN OLD MAN.

BUT, FOR BETTER OR WORSE, HE'S MY *DAD*, AND I'M THE ONLY ONE LEFT TO LOOK AFTER HIM. SO, I'D BEST SEE TO IT.

OLD FART PROBABLY JUST WANTED TO GET OFF *ALONE* SOMEWHERE, AWAY FROM EVERY- ONE WHO *HATES* HIM--WHICH IS PRETTY MUCH EVERYONE.

HE'LL TURN UP. WHERE'S HE GOING TO GO?

DO YOU THINK WE BURIED HIM *DEEP* ENOUGH?

I'LL WRITE UP THE ORDERS NOW.

BIGBY, CAN I TALK TO YOU FOR A MINUTE?

SURE, SHERIFF. WHAT'S UP?

WELL, THERE'S NO WAY TO *SUGAR-COAT* THIS, SO I'LL JUST SAY IT.

YOU NEED TO LEAVE THE FARM AREA.

WITH ALL OF THE RECENT TROUBLE, I'VE UNDERSTANDABLY *NOT* ENFORCED THE RULES AGAINST YOUR BEING HERE. BUT NOW WE'VE HAD A MOMENT TO CATCH OUR BREATH.

THIS PLACE CAN BE ENOUGH OF A POWDER KEG *WITHOUT* PROVOKING THE FARM FABLES BY LETTING YOU STAY HERE.

SO, HOW SOON CAN YOU HEAD BACK TO WOLF VALLEY?

ARE YOU *DONE*, SHERIFF? *MY* TURN TO SPEAK NOW?

LOOK, BIGBY, NO SENSE GETTING RILED AT *ME*. IT'S NOT *MY* RULE, IT'S WRITTEN INTO THE FARM'S *CONSTI-TUTION*.

IT WAS AN *UGLY* LITTLE LAW BACK THEN AND IT STILL IS TODAY. AND I'M *TIRED* OF IT.

YOU WANT TO KEEP THE FARM FREE OF DANGEROUS *KILLERS*? FINE! BUT DON'T SINGLE *ME* OUT.

NEXT: BIGBY AND BEAST THROW DOWN IN *THE GREAT FABLES CROSSOVER!*

RETURN TO THE JUNGLE BOOK

A Tale of Mowgli

HOMELAND RECOVERY

WOLF VALLEY.

SINCE THE WITCHING CLOAK IS OUT OF ACTION FOR NOW, FLYCATCHER HAS AGREED TO BE AT THE DESIGNATED EXTRACTION POINT.

HE'LL BE THERE FOR ONE *HOUR*, ON ONE DAY EACH WEEK, UNTIL *YOU* SHOW UP.

OR UNTIL YOU DECIDE WE MUST BE *DEAD?*

YES. OR UNTIL THEN.

JUST REMEMBER, THIS IS A JOURNEY OF *EXPLORATION*, TO SEE IF YOUR OLD JUNGLE HOME WORLD IS *VIABLE* FOR RECOLONIZATION.

SO DON'T MESS AROUND, MOWGLI. DON'T TREAT IT AS A VACATION HOMECOMING.

GET IN, HAVE A GOOD LONG LOOK, GATHER YOUR INTELLIGENCE, AND THEN GET *OUT*.

AVOID ALL CONTACT WITH EMPIRE FORCES, AND STAY SAFE.

OKAY, BUT YOU'RE TAKING ALL THE *FUN* OUT OF THIS TRIP, BIGBY.

I'M *SERIOUS.*

ANY IMPERIAL TROOPS STATIONED IN YOUR JUNGLE WORLD ARE LIKELY TO BE MORE DANGEROUS, NOW THAT THEY'RE CUT OFF FROM THEIR FORMER LEADERSHIP.

I KNOW, I KNOW. WE'LL BE CAREFUL AND DISCREET.

WE *PROMISE*, BOSS.

WELL, I'M NOT YOUR *BOSS* ANYMORE. I'M HAPPILY *RETIRED*, REMEMBER?

AREN'T YOU DIRECTOR OF HOMELAND RECOVERY NOW THAT PRINCE CHARMING IS DEAD?

OH, YEAH. SO, I GUESS I *AM* YOUR BOSS AGAIN. BUT I HOPE THIS IS JUST A TEMPORARY JOB. I EXPECT THE PRINCE MIGHT SURPRISE US ALL AND TURN UP AGAIN SOON.

WE UNDERSTAND.

YOU WON'T HAVE ANYTHING TO COMPLAIN ABOUT TO US, LITTLE BROTHER.

MAKE *DAMNED* SURE OF THAT.

NOW, HANG HERE FOR A MOMENT, WHILE I HAVE A CHAT WITH MY *REAL* FAMILY.

WE'RE GOING TO BE LEAVING SOON, SNOW.

YOU BOYS HAVE FUN.

DADDY! DADDY! DADDY! I HAVE A *QUESTION!*

NOT MUCH FUN FOR ME. I'M ONLY GOING AS FAR AS THE FARM'S BEANSTALK.

DADDY! DADDY! *DAAAAAA-DY!*

DADDY, WINTER HAS A QUESTION.

YES, WINTER, MY WEE DARLING?

DADDY...UHM...SOMEONE TOOK ALL OF OUR *GOLDFISH* AWAY. DO YOU KNOW WHERE THEY WENT?

YES, DEAR, THEY'RE RIGHT OVER THERE. THEY'RE WOLVES NOW--WELL, WOLF-*SHAPED*, ANYWAY.

SEE! I *TOLD* YOU THEY WERE OUR UNCLES ALL THE TIME! AND YOU CALLED ME A BIG FAT *LIAR!*

ONLY BECAUSE YOU LIE ABOUT EVERY-THING *ELSE!*

PLAY NICELY, MONSTERS, OR RECESS IS OVER AND IT'S BACK TO THE *MATH* BOOKS.

-tick-tick-sprong-tick-

GOOD AFTERNOON TO YOU, GENTLE-*tck*-CREATURES. ALLOW ME TO INTRODUCE MY-*tck*-SELF.

I AM LORD *MOUNTBATTEN*, LAST-*tck*-LAST-*tck*-LAST VICEROY OF THE RAJ.

AND MAY I ALSO PRESENT *BAD SAM* (WHO'S NOT AT ALL A BAD FELLOW, ACTUALLY), MY-*tck*-MY LAST LOYAL SEPOY.

PLEEESHED T'MAKE Y'QUAINTENSH, I'M *SHHHURE*.

HUH?

NEXT:
THE LEGEND OF
LORD MOUNTBATTEN.

162

WOLF MANOR.

YOU *LEFT* THEM THERE, MOWGLI?

WHO *AUTHORIZED* THAT?

I DID.

THE FORMER EMPIRE TROOPS STILL OCCUPYING THE AREA ARE PRETTY DISPIRITED, DISORGANIZED AND *LEADERLESS* JUST NOW.

BUT LEAVE THEM ALONE FOR A FEW MORE WEEKS, OR MONTHS, AND THEY *MIGHT* GET THEIR ACT TOGETHER.

SO I EXERCISED SOME INITIATIVE AS THE RANKING OFFICER IN THE FIELD AND ALLOWED YOUR SIX BROTHERS TO DO WHAT THEY *MOST* WANTED TO DO.

STAY BEHIND AND SOW FEAR, SABOTAGE, DEATH AND DESTRUCTION AMONG THE ENEMY.

WHICH THEY TURNED OUT TO BE QUITE *GOOD* AT, BY THE WAY.

THIS WAS SUPPOSED TO BE STRICTLY A *RECON* MISSION.

IT WUSH AND WE ⸢HIC⸣ DID, MON-SHWAR. AND AN *EXSHELLENT* JOB WE DID TOO, IF I MUSHT SAY.

WHO--?

BIGBY, MAY I INTRODUCE TWO NEW FRIENDS AND ALLIES IN THE STRUGGLE?

THIS IS MOUNTBATTEN, LORD VICEROY OF THE INDU WORLD AND COMMANDER OF ALL FORCES OF THE RAJ.

BUT YOU CAN JOLLY WELL CALL ME *MONTY*.

I UNDERSTAND WITH SO MANY KINGS, SATRAPS, PRINCES AND PRINCESSES MAKING UP *YOU* LOT OF EXILED FABLES--

--WE DON'T STAND MUCH ON *CEREMONY* HERE.

AND THIS IS BAD SAM, HIS--WELL, I GUESS YOU'D SAY SAM WAS THE ENTIRETY OF MONTY'S ARMY.

I'M FEW IN NUMBERS, BUT *FIERSH*, GOOD SIR!

AS THE RIGHTFUL HEIR OF THE INDU, MONTY HAD THE AUTHORITY TO ALLOW BAGHEERA AND YOUR BROTHERS TO REMAIN BEHIND AND CONTINUE THE FIGHT FOR LIBERATION.

OR ACTUALLY *BEGIN* THE FIGHT, IF YOU WANT TO GET TECHNICAL.

"YOU SHOULD HAVE *SEEN* THEM, BIGBY. SUCH FEARSOME *MONSTERS* THEY BECAME! THE GOB ENCAMPMENTS SCATTERED TO THE FOUR WINDS!"

RUN, YOU PUNY WARRIOR GOBS!

THROW DOWN YOUR ARMS AND *FLEE* OUR HOME!

GO FIND YOURSELVES MORE *PEACEFUL* JOBS!

OR WE'LL MAKE A *STEW* OF YOUR FLESH AND BONE!

OKAY, SOME OF HIS DIALOGUE WAS A *BIT* LESS THAN A HUNDRED PERCENT AUTHENTIC, BUT THESE GOBS WEREN'T EXACTLY THE BRIGHTEST TOOLS IN THE BOX.

IT SEEMS THE CRÈME OF THE EMPIRE'S FORCES DON'T GET ASSIGNED GARRISON DUTY ON A REMOTE, UNIMPORTANT WORLD LIKE THE INDU.

UNIMPORTANT? *WITHDRAW* THAT BRAZEN IMPERTINENCE THIS *INSTANT!*

SORRY, MONTY. NO OFFENSE INTENDED.

THE POINT, BIGBY, IS THAT THEIR IMPERFECT ACT WAS CREDIBLE ENOUGH FOR OUR *NEEDS.*

IF WE MOVE *FAST,* WE CAN TAKE THE ENTIRETY OF THE INDU BACK EASILY.

BUT IF WE WAIT UNTIL THE GOBS RETURN, OR SOME *NEW* THUG DECIDES TO MOVE INTO THE POWER VACUUM...

OKAY, YOU'VE *CONVINCED* ME. WE'LL SET UP A MEETING WITH SOME OF THE MORE *INVASION-HAPPY* MEMBERS OF OUR DECOMMISSIONED ARMY.

ASSUMING YOU WANT A *REAL* ARMY, VICEROY, I'VE GOT ONE THAT I NEED TO FIND WORK FOR.

BUT FIRST THINGS FIRST. FLY, YOU'RE ABOUT TO BE LATE FOR HAULING THE FIRST WAVE OF FABLES TO BLUE'S SERVICE. AND YOU'RE NOT EVEN *DRESSED* YET.

OH, OF COURSE. I'LL BE BACK IN TWO SHAKES.

SERVICE? WHAT *SORT* OF SERVICE IS BLUE GETTING? ANOTHER WAR MEDAL?

NOT *QUITE,* MOWG. LET'S GO INSIDE AND SEE IF WE CAN'T FIND A SUIT THAT WILL FIT YOU.

AND THEN I'LL CATCH YOU UP ON THE LATEST NEWS.

THE END (of a sort)